Canyons and Lakes

of Grand Teton National Park

Written by
Charles Craighead

Photography by
Henry H. Holdsworth

Official Guidebook
of Grand Teton National Park

Published by
Grand Teton Natural History Association

Table *of* Contents

Tetons from the east shore of Jackson Lake

Canyons and Lakes of Grand Teton National Park

Featuring Jenny Lake and Cascade Canyon

The abrupt rise of the twelve central peaks of the Tetons never fails to draw a visitor's gaze upward to the windswept summits and is undoubtedly the reason this area became a national park in 1929. The Tetons continue to capture the immediate attention of all who come here, but other geologic features of the mountains play a big part in making them unique, both in their beauty and in their diverse natural history.

In addition to their sheer rise without foothills, the individual peaks stand clearly apart from each other. Unlike many mountain ranges, the peaks are in full view and identifiable from almost any angle, even from neighboring Idaho. Over the mountains' 9 million year history, ice, water, and gravity have gradually chiseled away at the rock. The hardest rock forms the core group of peaks, so they have weathered and eroded the least. A series of breathtaking summits remains, but so does a series of equally grand spaces between the summits.

As artists and photographers know, the empty spaces around subjects can accentuate them, and in the Teton Range these empty spaces are the many glacier-carved canyons. They give definition to the peaks and they set geologic formations apart. But canyons aren't just empty air; they are also rich and interesting worlds in themselves. What the canyon-forming glaciers took away in rock, they gave back in diversity including moraines, lakes, streams, and alpine meadows.

Unlike the peaks, whose names read like a list of early explorers or lofty descriptions, the names of the canyons reflect the more poetic side of geography: Granite, Open, Death, Avalanche, Garnet, Cascade, Paintbrush. If the summit of the Grand Teton gives us a place to view the whole world, then Death Canyon offers a place to sit and reflect on the need to preserve the natural beauty of that world.

Native Americans and mountain men of the 1800s saw canyons as a way to pass through a mountain range. Later adventurers found that the canyons provided access to routes up the peaks. Today, canyons are often themselves a destination. Each canyon in the Tetons evolved its own character and its own appeal: a view, a waterfall, a lake, or an alpine meadow. Often the appeal is harder to pin down; it may be the enclosed feeling from the peaks looming above, the soft echo of mountain songbirds, or the play of shadows and light on the canyon walls. Many park visitors who set out to hike long miles to a backcountry destination find contentment in just exploring the canyon trails. A mountain canyon can be the ideal place to escape from the world for a day.

Most of the Tetons' canyons are accessible by maintained trails, but others are considered a part of the more sensitive backcountry, and travel into them is not encouraged. They can still be enjoyed from a distance, as part of the overall scenery. The appeal of these canyons actually lies in their emptiness, almost as if they are open windows into the mountains.

The Tetons' array of glacial lakes also helps set them apart. A dozen lakes lie right at the foot of the mountains and on the valley floor, and twice that many are sprinkled throughout the Tetons. They vary from the deep and expansive Jackson Lake at the foot of Mount Moran to tiny alpine jewels like Holly Lake, high in Paintbrush Canyon. Lakes have always had a magical air about them, and when they occur in contrast to the stark mountains above they are especially beautiful.

In general, the lakes at the base of the Tetons are the largest. Formed by glaciers that advanced out of the canyons about 15,000 years ago, they occupy deep depressions in the valley floor. Soil and rocks carried out of the mountains by ice were deposited at their terminal ends, building up berms called moraines. When the glaciers eventually melted back into the mountains, they left lakes rimmed with higher ground. Geologists call these piedmont lakes. Phelps, Jenny, Leigh, Taggart, and Bradley lakes are piedmont lakes, each uniquely paired with the canyon they are associated with; they are still fed by streams from their respective canyons. Their flat, blue surfaces hug the base of the Tetons and help to emphasize the abruptness of the mountains. On a calm morning they may reflect a mirror image of the peaks.

Most of the high alpine lakes can be found at the head of a canyon in a rugged cirque scooped out by a glacier. Cold, relatively barren little lakes that are frozen over and buried under snow in their cirques for half the year, they are logically called cirque lakes. During the warmer months they become the prime destination of hikers, campers, photographers, and artists when alpine wildflowers line their shores, and they reflect the surrounding mountain scenery.

Each lake in Grand Teton National Park has its own appeal. Some are ideal for a quiet day in a canoe, some are perfect for an hour of trout fishing, and others offer an invigorating swim on a warm afternoon. Like the canyons, the lakes range from those that are open for visitor activities to those that should only be visited occasionally and with great care.

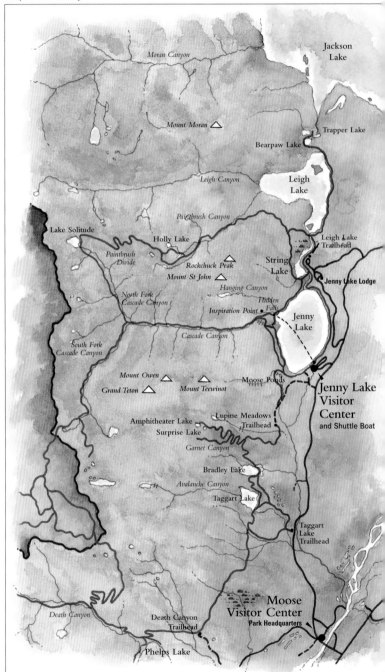

View of Cascade Canyon across Jenny Lake

Cascade Canyon & Jenny Lake

The largest and most accessible canyon in the park, Cascade Canyon divides the peaks of Grand Teton National Park down the middle. It leads directly and gently to the heart of the mountains, where it splits and offers routes north and south into the backcountry. Cascade Canyon blends spectacular views, easy hiking, a beautiful mountain stream, alpine meadows, wildlife, and wildflowers. Since Grand Teton National Park was first established, Cascade Canyon has been one of its best known and most visited areas.

The ancient glacier that scoured and shaped Cascade Canyon also flowed out of the mountains to carve a deep lake at the mouth of the canyon. Glaciers move downhill as a result of their sheer mass, and they are constantly breaking up and melting at the bottom while compaction of new snow at the top creates more ice. The combined weight and pushing power of the glacier created Jenny Lake. Together, Cascade Canyon and Jenny Lake now form the center of visitor activity in Grand Teton National Park.

The view from the wooded eastern shore of Jenny Lake, across the expanse of sparkling water and up Cascade Canyon to the Tetons' highest peaks, easily sums up the grandeur of Grand Teton National Park. It was here on the shores of Jenny Lake that inspiration came to many of those who worked to protect the landscape for posterity.

Jenny Lake

The period of glaciation forming the raw shapes of Cascade Canyon and Jenny Lake ended about 14,000 years ago, and the huge depression in the ground occupied by the terminal end of the Cascade glacier filled with melting ice to become a lake. The slightly higher ground rimming the lake came from the conveyor-belt-like activity of the glacier as it carried and pushed its accumulated soil and rock out of the canyon. This moraine wasn't necessary to create the lake, since the ground was already deeply gouged, but the moraine held back the melting ice and shaped the shoreline. More important, all the soil, clay, and other ground-up material of the moraine held moisture and gave plants a more fertile place to take root. Even today the glacial moraine of Jenny Lake stands out with its markedly different vegetation.

Jenny Lake is approximately two miles long, a little over a mile wide, and over 200 feet to the bottom at its deepest point, toward the west (mountain) side of the lake. Two inlets feed it: one where Cascade Creek tumbles out of Cascade Canyon and empties into the west side of the lake; and another

Mount Moran from Jenny Lake

where String Lake just to the north drains to form a picturesque stream that also flows into Jenny Lake. The lake's outlet is named Cottonwood Creek.

The glacial moraine containing Jenny Lake forms the slight rise between the parking area and the lake. Compared to the flat, sagebrush-covered land just to the east, the moraine seems like an eden of Lodgepole Pine and aspen trees, grass, shrubs, and wildflowers. The glacial silt and clay hold water much better than the loose cobble of the valley floor and provide a nourishing site for plant growth.

Scattered all over the moraine you can see rocks and boulders that look almost as if they were dropped from the sky. These erratics, as geologists call them, were carried by the glaciers and dropped here as the ice melted. Mountain climbers use a few of the larger ones to hone their skills.

A Brief History of Jenny Lake

Grand Teton National Park was set aside for its natural beauty and wild state, but parts of it have a rich human history as well. The first Native Americans showed up even as the glaciers were disappearing; early stone artifacts date back to 11,000 years ago. At that time the valley floor probably looked more like alpine tundra, without trees or sagebrush.

Indians visited the valley regularly until the early 1800s, when the first white explorers showed up. Although the Indians certainly named many places, the explorers and survey parties renamed everything from their own civilization. This picturesque lake at the base of the Tetons was named "Jenny Lake" by the Hayden survey expedition of 1872 after Jenny Leigh, the wife of Jackson Hole explorer and guide "Beaver Dick" Leigh. Leigh Lake just to the north also bears their name.

While the Teton Range and its canyons, including Cascade Canyon, were protected by various federal conservation acts of the late 1800s, the sur-rounding flats were briefly opened for homesteading in the early 1920s. Several homesteaders claimed prime land around Jenny Lake, knowing full well that the land's scenic value far outweighed its meager ability to support agriculture. Over the years people tried to make a go of dude ranches, dance halls, cabins, campgrounds, boat rentals, gas stations, and general stores. With the establishment of Grand Teton National Park in 1929, those homestead properties around the lake became even more valuable.

The rush to develop and commercialize Jenny Lake prompted an intensive property buy-up by the Rockefeller family under the name of the "Snake River Land Company," with the goal of removing the buildings and eventu-ally preserving the land as a park. Their effort, although misunderstood and distrusted at the time, was responsible for today's uncluttered roadways and low-key development.

Homesteaders who staked claims here in the 1800s prized the lands along Cottonwood Creek. Much of the development occurred in this area south of the lake's outlet, and most of the cabins and barns at Lupine Meadows, at the Climber's Ranch, and next to the creek on the road to Moose mark these places of historical use. Jenny Lake Lodge, the only other development in the area, began as the Danny Ranch and was purchased by the Snake River Land Company in the 1930s. It was eventually restored as a rustic inn. The Jenny Lake Visitor Center was formerly the Harrison Crandall Studio, which was itself built from the logs of a dance pavilion built and later torn down by Crandall.

Present-day services are limited to a few necessary National Park Service buildings and seasonal park concessions. Many of the original homestead buildings were moved and incorporated into the new park after it was opened.

Mount Teewinot from the east shore of Jenny Lake (right)

Jenny Lake Visitor Center

Activities

One of the reasons Jenny Lake remains so popular is the variety of activities originating here. Many of the park's premier backcountry hikes start nearby; the boat service carries visitors across the lake, and the Jenny Lake campground fills up all summer. The South Jenny Lake area has a tradition of being the heart of the park's mountaineering and backcountry activities, dating back to the first summer Grand Teton was open. But Jenny Lake is also a great place to stroll along the lakeshore trails to look for wildflowers and wildlife, learn a bit of history, or just sit and watch the constantly shifting light on the lake and mountains.

Facilities and Services

Jenny Lake Boat Dock

Parking: During the off-season or very early in the day, the extensive parking areas near Jenny Lake may seem out of proportion to the limited facilities. However, the area's proximity to so many wonderful places helps draw a large percentage of the park's visitors. On any given day hikers, boaters, climbers, fishermen, photographers, and every other sort of visitor use the area.

Jenny Lake Visitor Center: Interpretive exhibits, photographs, maps, and books help to give visitors a detailed understanding of the area.

Jenny Lake Store: The Jenny Lake Store provides a few basic necessities for hikers and visitors, as well as interpretive material, maps, and books.

Jenny Lake Ranger Station: Tucked back in the trees behind the store and the visitor center sits the Jenny Lake Ranger Station. Backcountry campers, mountain climbers, and hikers get information and permits here, apply for campsites, and learn of the latest conditions in the mountains.

Campground: Nestled in the pine trees north of the facilities, the Jenny Lake Campground remains the most popular campground in the park and requires some persistence and timing in registering for a site. This campground is reserved for tent camping only.

Boat Dock: At the south end of Jenny Lake, the cold, clear water flows out to create Cottonwood Creek, which winds its way for about seven miles across the sagebrush flats to reach the Snake River. The slightly protected cove where Cottonwood Creek begins was the logical place to launch rowboats in the early days, and by 1924 visitors rented small rowboats here. This site evolved into the present-day boat dock and shuttle service to Cascade Canyon. The boats run daily from May through September, ferrying hikers across the lake for a fee.

Exum Guide Service: Just downstream of the boat dock another wooden footbridge crosses Cottonwood Creek. This bridge leads to the Exum Guide Service and on to Lupine Meadows beyond. The Exum Guide Service was founded by climbers Glenn Exum and Paul Petzoldt in the 1930s. Today it still offers professional instruction in climbing techniques and mountaineering safety, as well as guided ascents of all the peaks.

Jenny Lake Trail

Next to the East Shore Boat Dock, a footbridge crosses the creek and leads off toward the mountains. This marks the beginning of the Jenny Lake Loop trail around the lake. The trail also follows the shoreline of the lake in the opposite direction, and the two meet up at the String Lake Bridge to the north. On the west side of the lake, the trail branches off to Hidden Falls, Inspiration Point, and Cascade Canyon.

Moose Ponds, just up the trail from the boat dock, is found on a short route that loops around the ponds and back to the parking area through Lupine Meadows. You can watch for moose, beaver, and other wildlife from the overlook on the main trail and then return to the bridge and boat dock.

The Jenny Lake Loop, which circles the lake in just under seven easy miles, was the first trail constructed in the park, back in 1930. At the West Side Boat Dock, this trail forks off to Cascade Canyon. From the north end of Jenny Lake, trails lead to String Lake, Leigh Lake, and Paintbrush Canyon.

Fishing

Jenny Lake provides fishing all year for the three species of trout inhabiting the lake. It requires a Wyoming fishing license, available at various outlets within the park. Regulations restrict fishing to artificial lures (no bait) and limit the size and number of trout that may be kept. You'll find the current regulations at the park's visitor centers.

Jenny Lake Trail

Most fishing in Jenny Lake is done from the rocky shore with fly rod or spinning gear. The inlets are popular spots, especially the scenic little stream entering from String Lake, but the outlet of the lake where Cottonwood Creek begins, by the boat dock, stays closed to fishing year-round.

Fishing by boat is also permitted on Jenny Lake, but motors are not allowed. Canoes, rowboats, and kayaks can be launched from the shoreline at a small launch site just west of the shuttle boat dock. You can only reach this launch site from the Lupine Meadows Road, a mile south of the South Jenny Lake area. A park boat permit is required and available at the ranger station.

Winter road closures requiring an eight-mile round trip on skis limit winter ice fishing on Jenny Lake. The National Park Service enforces a number of safety regulations for boating on the lakes in Grand Teton, and this informa-tion is provided when you obtain a boat permit from the ranger station. Jenny Lake is deep and cold, and despite its relatively small size it can have extremely rough water during a sudden wind storm. The prevailing weather comes over the mountains toward the lake and often surprises boaters on the open water.

Swimming

Swimming is not permitted in Jenny Lake. However, it is a welcome activity just to the north in String Lake, which is much shallower and warmer.

Bull moose

Wildlife

Moose are members of the deer family and browse on the twigs and shoots of shrubs. They also eat aquatic vegetation, wading shoulder-deep in water. Look for moose early and late in the day at Moose Ponds, along the shore of the lake and on the steep lower slopes of the nearby Teewinot Mountain.

Bird-watchers can spend endless days around Jenny Lake, sitting under a pine tree by the lakeshore or walking the trails early in the morning. Look for Common Loons and Western Grebes out on the open water of the lake, and for the Western Tanager in the Lodgepole Pines. The friendly Gray Jay inhabits pine trees near the ranger station and throughout the campground.

In the shrubs along the shoreline, look for the bright little Yellow Warbler and listen to its cheery song. It flits out of the brush to catch insects in the air, and it nests in willow thickets.

Mountain Bluebirds, Lazuli Buntings, and various warblers summer in the mixed vegetation and open meadows around the lakeshore, especially at the south end. Walking the Moose Ponds loop and returning to Jenny Lake

Male Mountain Bluebird

through Lupine Meadows and along Cottonwood Creek will always produce bird sightings.

Ospreys are large fish-eating birds of prey. Seasonal residents of the park, they build a large stick platform nest, usually on top of a dead tree, and return to the same nest year after year. Several Osprey pairs nest in the Jenny Lake area, and the adult birds often circle over the lake while hunting. Occasionally, a Bald Eagle will try to intimidate the Osprey into dropping its catch.

Black bears are fairly common around Jenny Lake, most often seen off the trail eating berries or other vegetation. Females with cubs occasionally spend their days in the forest on the western shores of the lake. Black bears can also be spotted at dawn and at dusk on the lower slopes of Mount Teewinot. Moose Ponds and Lupine Meadows offer great views of that part of the mountain.

Beaver feeding

Beavers live largely nocturnal lives, but in the short summer of the Tetons they often come out late in the day. Moose Ponds is a likely spot to watch, especially if you're returning from a hike in late afternoon.

Marmots, ground squirrels, red squirrels, and chipmunks all live in the Jenny Lake area. They have adapted to park structures and can often be seen perched on log parking barriers, peering out from underneath buildings, or running along the wooden fences.

Elk can often be seen in Lupine Meadows at the south end of Jenny Lake. They spend the day bedded down in the Lodgepole Pine forest and come out in the evening. Their calves are born in late May or early June. By mid-September the bull elk are "bugling" as their mating season peaks.

Mule deer thrive in the park and can be found in all habitat types. They are most common in mixed forests of aspen and pine, and in open meadows.

Pronghorn, commonly called antelope, inhabit the open areas of Lupine Meadows and the sagebrush flats along the Teton Park Road in summer. They migrate out of the Jackson Hole valley for the winter.

Wildflowers

Wildflowers high in the Tetons

Regulations prohibit picking any wildflowers in a national park, so you may see them thriving just about anywhere, even in islands in the parking lots. Look for the plentiful yellow blossoms of Arrowleaf Balsamroot in early summer and the similar Mules Ear with shiny, darker green leaves later on. Wildflowers appear seasonally, and in the short alpine summers one species may only bloom for a few weeks and then wither. However, the blooms arrive later as elevation increases, so you can often find flowers in the mountains that are already past bloom in the valley.

Many of the flowering berry bushes such as Huckleberry, Twinberry, Bearberry, and Serviceberry grow along the lakeshore and under the pines. Along the trail loop, under aspen and pine trees, look for columbine and geranium. In open meadows, watch for the Showy Green Gentian. On the cool, shaded west side of the lake on the trail to the boat dock Bog-orchids and Fairyslippers appear briefly in early summer.

Lupine Meadows, a short walk from the South Jenny Lake parking area, lives up to its name. In June and early July, Silvery Lupine blankets the meadow. Mixed in with the sagebrush in Lupine Meadows you might find Indian Paintbrush, Balsamroot, or Larkspur. Early season visitors will see the brief blooms of Yellow Violet, Shooting Star, and Yellow Bell.

Trees

Aspens in fall

The tall, thin, and stately pines growing all around the Jenny Lake area are Lodgepole Pines. Mixed in on the east side of the lake, usually out in the open, an occasional Douglas Fir or a Limber Pine grows. Aspen trees create small stands on the south end of the lake and on the lower slopes of Mount Teewinot. Along Cottonwood Creek grow, of course, cottonwood trees. On the west side of the lake where there is more moisture and more shade, Engelmann Spruce form the tallest stands of trees in the park.

Wild Blue Flax (left)

Geology

The Teton Fault scarp

The geologic processes that shaped this present landscape near Jenny Lake left lots of clues to their actions, and over the years geologists have pieced together the story. In a nutshell, two large blocks of the earth were split by a fault now marked by the north-south base of the Tetons. Today, the Teton Fault reveals its continuing activity in a visible scarp on the steep hillside just above String Lake. The fault scarp is best viewed from the Cathedral Group Turnout on the road heading into String Lake.

As forces deeper in the earth moved the blocks, the east side of the fault dropped down while the west side lifted up. This process took millions of years, but eventually a 30,000-foot difference stood between the two sides of the fault. The resulting mountains on the west side, the Tetons, weathered and eroded through several ice ages and periods of local glaciers to reach their present appearance. Huge glaciers from the north and east scoured the entire valley, and when they eventually melted away they left enough rock debris to fill in and level the tilted valley floor. More material came from uplifted land to the northwest.

This all occurred fairly recently, to a geologist's thinking anyway. The Tetons are still relatively fresh. Most of the mountain uplift has happened in the last five million years, while the rest of the Rockies are about 60 million years old. The Tetons still rise, and the valley still sinks.

The many periods of glacial activity and individual glaciers overlapped and tended to cover up or wipe out the work of previous ones. Basically, the valley floor comprises all kinds of material left from the large glaciers that came from the north, while the moraines around the lakes came from later glaciers in the mountains. The present-day small glaciers high in the Tetons began to form only about 1,000 years ago.

At the time the large glaciers began to melt, very little soil and no plants or animals existed in the valley. Ice had scoured it clean, and much of what soil remained got washed down the prehistoric Snake River channels by melting ice. So the valley of Jackson Hole started from scratch, but the process of building soil and establishing new plants began even as the ice retreated. Wind-blown dirt accumulated, plants worked their way back into the valley from outside and spread down from the alpine areas above the glaciers, and eventually animals were able to survive.

Snow melting in the high country (left)

Grand Teton from north fork of Cascade Canyon

Cascade Canyon

Many visitors to Grand Teton National Park find Cascade Canyon almost a complete park experience in itself. Unsurpassed scenery, fascinating geology, and encounters with wildlife make it possible to experience a cross-section of the park's features in one place.

Only one trail leads up the canyon, but it can be reached by several routes. The Jenny Lake Trail circles Jenny Lake, and near the West Shore Boat Dock it branches off to connect with the Cascade Canyon Trail. The Jenny Lake Trail can be accessed easily at either the Jenny Lake parking area or at the String Lake parking area; the distance and difficulty are about the same either way.

Riding the shuttle boat across the lake from the East Shore Boat Dock saves the 2-mile walk around the lake, although it also bypasses a very pretty part of the trail following the contours of the lake. Some hikers prefer to warm up for their day in Cascade Canyon by hiking around the lake and then riding the shuttle back later in the day when those last two miles can seem much longer.

Horses are allowed on the Cascade Canyon Trail, and they offer a means of travel into the backcountry for visitors unable to hike. Horse parties may depart from String Lake Trailhead or Lupine Meadows. Near the West Shore Boat Dock there's a separate horse trail for the first half-mile to Hidden Falls.

Hidden Falls (left)

Jenny Lake from Inspiration Point

Hidden Falls

Hidden Falls

Probably the most visited hiking destination in the park, Hidden Falls cascades over a high rock face just a short half-mile up the Cascade Canyon Trail from the West Shore Boat Dock. The 200-foot high falls are hidden in the trees and surrounding rocks, but you can often hear them before you get there. Early in the season, when melting snow fills Cascade Creek to overflowing, Hidden Falls creates an especially spectacular scene. Even when visitors are numerous, the thundering water, mist, and beauty make it possible to tune out everything but the waterfalls.

The short but steep hike from the boat dock to Hidden Falls winds along Cascade Creek as it plunges the last few hundred feet to Jenny Lake. The fast moving water of this rugged stretch of the creek supports the unique habits of American Dippers, little water-proof birds that walk underwater and eat insect larvae. Another bird at home in the turbulent Cascade Creek, the strikingly marked Harlequin Duck, arrives here in late spring after wintering on the Pacific Ocean.

Inspiration Point

Less than a half-mile up the trail from Hidden Falls you'll find Inspiration Point. The steep trail to it cuts across a rock face to level out on top of a rocky knob. If the trail to Hidden Falls seemed filled with hikers, you can count on this section of trail to thin the crowds. From Inspiration Point, expansive views of Jenny Lake, the Jackson Hole valley, and the mountains beyond unfold. The pine-covered glacial moraine forming Jenny Lake is easily distinguished from the surrounding landscape. Inspiration Point marks another turnaround spot, so beyond this point the hiker numbers may again decrease.

Cascade Canyon

Upper Cascade Canyon Trail

Cascade Canyon really begins where the trail leaves Inspiration Point, and it runs almost due west for 3.5 miles before splitting into two smaller canyons. The trail climbs very gradually as it works its way through all kinds of habitat, from boulder fields to conifer forests to lush little meadows. The canyon feels wide, airy, and beautiful, and all the while the peaks of the Tetons loom overhead. Immediately to the south rises the flank of Teewinot Mountain, but the rugged Mount Owen, second highest peak in the Tetons, dominates the skyline. As the trail continues, the Grand Teton will emerge from behind Mount Owen. To the right, or north side of the canyon looms Storm Point and above that, Mount St. John. You can't tell from the trail on the canyon floor, but Cascade Canyon forms a fairly symmetrical U-shape which points to its glacial origins. Eventually the trail splits, one fork leading off to the north to Lake Solitude, and the other going south toward Hurricane Pass.

Camping

Regulations prohibit camping in Cascade Canyon until you pass the fork in the trail where the canyon divides. Here, established camping zones and a permit system allow visitors to enjoy the canyon overnight. Permits need to be obtained ahead of time from rangers at the visitor centers.

Wildlife

Black bear and cub

Canyons in general create ideal habitat for wildlife, and Cascade Canyon is no exception. Somewhat protected from the weather and warmer than the surrounding mountains, it offers wildlife a diversity of habitat and vegetation. Over the thousands of years since the last major glaciers melted, the rocky canyon floor gradually collected areas of soil as material weathered off the surrounding walls and blew in on the wind. Eventually, large plants could grow, and the mix of vegetation now supports many wild animal species.

Moose inhabit Cascade Canyon from early spring through late fall. They browse on willow shoots and other woody plants as well as eating sedges and aquatic plants. In Cascade Canyon moose tend to stay near the creek, feeding in the willow thickets or bedded down under the conifers. Moose can be unpredictably aggressive, especially a cow with her calf, and should always be given a wide berth. Only the bulls grow antlers, which they shed in late winter.

Black bears spend summers in Cascade Canyon, but are not numerous. They are creatures of habit, so park rangers can usually tell you where bears have been seen. Black bears eat mostly plants, but whenever opportunities arise they will kill game or feed on a dead animal. They are not considered a threat to humans unless they've become accustomed to hikers' food, and then they can be aggressive.

The plaintive little bleat that seems to come from piles of rock along the trail actually comes from a small mammal called the pika, related to hares and rabbits. Pikas are fascinating animals that spend the summer storing grass and forbs in little haystacks so they can eat through the long winter.

A number of other small mammals live in the canyon and are often seen along the trail. Chipmunks, golden-mantled ground squirrels, and red squirrels are most common. A much larger rodent, the marmot, likes to bask in the sun on top of a rock. Marmots may be either golden brown or jet black.

Birds seen in the canyon vary with the vegetation, habitat, season, and time of day. The most common species include the American Dipper, sparrows, and warblers along Cascade Creek; Stellar's and Gray jays, Mountain Chickadees and juncos in the conifer forests; and ravens flying overhead.

Bull moose in velvet (left)

Wildflowers in Cascade Canyon

Wildflowers and Trees

Plant life changes gradually with the elevation as you hike up Cascade Canyon. The plants become smaller and hardier as you climb, but local differences in soil, moisture, temperature, and sunlight also affect their growth. In the lower parts of the canyon, especially around Hidden Falls, grow tall Englemann Spruce that may be 400 years old. On drier sites, around Inspiration Point and on the south-facing side of the canyon, Lodgepole Pines and Douglas Fir trees are common. Subalpine Fir begins to join the mix of fir and pine as you go up the trail, and eventually the Whitebark Pines show up as the others drop off. The Whitebark Pines and Limber Pines are hardy, high altitude trees, but even they get more stunted and twisted as you climb.

Flowers also reflect the changes that higher elevations bring, and they tend to get smaller and grow closer to the ground as you go up. Wildflowers are a subject in themselves, and the best way to appreciate them is to carry a wildflower book and stop to identify the plants as you go. As the trail begins in the cool shade near Jenny Lake, columbines, geraniums, Silky Phacelia, and Fairyslippers may be in bloom.

Once you climb past Hidden Falls and out into the open canyon, all kinds of flowers appear. You may see Yellow Monkeyflowers growing next to the creek or Parry Primroses among the rocks. When the trail winds through conifers, there are Mountain Ash and Honeysuckle plants. After the fork in the trail at the head of Cascade Canyon, smaller but brilliant subalpine flowers such as Paintbrush, Saxifrage, Spirea, Moss Campion, and Marsh Marigold grow.

Looking up Cascade Canyon from Inspiration Point (right)

Fox Creek Pass, upper Granite Canyon

Canyons with Well-Maintained Trails

When you look at the full length of the Teton Range from one of the scenic turnouts along the park highway, it's obvious that there are two basic kinds of canyons: the deep, major ones that appear to cut completely through the mountain range, and the smaller, shallower ones that lead up into the higher elevations.

Four major canyons in the park have maintained trails:Granite, Death, Cascade, and Paintbrush. Three other major canyons—Avalanche, Leigh, and Moran—are not accessible by maintained trails, although unofficial, "social" trails do exist. Numerous other named canyons, draws, and gulches are spread throughout the Tetons, but only two are generally accessible by maintained trails. They are Open Canyon, toward the south end of the park, and Garnet Canyon, next to the Grand Teton. For the most part, park trails were first established where traditional use occurred, so they provide access to the most popular and most scenic areas, as well as to destinations such as lakes and waterfalls.

Besides the popular Cascade Canyon, the following five canyons have developed trails. All are different, and each provides a unique experience in Grand Teton. Their main similarity is easy access; in most cases you enter the canyon within an hour of leaving the trailhead. Their attractions range from spectacular scenery to pristine lakes to wild solitude.

Granite Canyon

Upper Granite Canyon, trail to Marion Lake

The southernmost canyon in the park, Granite Canyon, has lush vegetation, dense stands of trees, and wildflowers. It also has one of the newest trails in the park. You reach Granite Canyon from the Granite Canyon Trailhead on the Moose-Wilson Road, or from the aerial tram at Teton Village. The tram makes this area popular because it does the climbing for you, and most of the hike back to the Granite Canyon Trailhead is then downhill.

Snow melts fairly early in Granite so its trails are some of the first to open for the hiking season. The south wall shows lots of signs of the canyon's winter conditions: steep avalanche chutes, piles of snow, and broken trees. Granite Creek flows down the canyon and out between high granite walls that give the canyon its name. Upper Granite Canyon, with its sedimentary rocks, came from a different geologic background than canyons near the main peaks. It offers open camping, except near the mouth of the canyon and close to the National Park Service patrol cabin. Deer and moose are a common sight in Granite, and an occasional black bear inhabits the canyon. Marion Lake, near the head of the canyon, makes a popular backcountry destination.

Open Canyon

Trails from Death Canyon Parking or Granite Canyon Parking access Open

Open Canyon

Canyon. It can also be reached on a long route from the aerial tram at Teton Village. The trail up Open Canyon presents a fairly difficult hike, but it offers virtual solitude, a different geology, and quiet camping. It provides backcountry access to peaks and lakes in the area, but does not have a popular destination within its walls.

A fault that runs east-west up the bottom of Open Canyon marks the geologic boundary between two parts of the Teton Range. Land to the south sank, and its formations are largely sedimentary rock. To the north, the land rose and the sedimentary rock eroded to reveal the hard metamorphic rock of the present-day Teton peaks.

Death Canyon

Death Canyon

One of the most striking canyons, with its sheer walls seeming to guard the entrance to the backcountry, Death Canyon has the oldest trail in the park, built in 1920-21. The most beautiful access is also the shortest, starting at the Death Canyon Trailhead and going up and over the high moraine to Phelps Lake. Even if you don't go any farther, the view from the overlook on top of the moraine makes the hike worth it. Unlike the terminal moraine at Jenny Lake, this lateral moraine formed along the edge of the glacier. The trail follows Death Creek up to a patrol cabin, and then divides. The Alaska Basin Trail branches off here and crosses over the divide between Static Peak and Horace Albright Peak.

Black bears like Death Canyon in the summer, but they're usually seen off trail. Beyond the patrol cabin the trail gets more difficult and steep in places. It winds through spruce and fir stands and climbs through meadows for a view of the Death Canyon Shelf. The south side (north-facing) has dense trees because of snow accumulation in winter. The trail continues on up through meadow, willows, and wildflowers to Fox Creek Pass.

Garnet Canyon

Garnet Canyon

The Garnet Canyon Trail, accessed from the Lupine Meadows Trailhead, is used primarily by mountaineers headed up to climb the Grand Teton, South Teton, or Middle Teton peaks. The trail veers off from the Amphitheater Lake Trail and contours around the face of the mountain slope to enter Garnet Canyon. Garnet Creek winds below and empties into Bradley Lake. The trail offers great views of the valley below and the peaks looming over the canyon. The trail ends in a field of boulders, beyond which backcountry experience and skills are necessary.

Along the way, marmots and pikas can usually be seen on the rocky slopes beside the trail. Before the trail enters Garnet Canyon there are abundant wildflowers growing on the open hillside.

Trail in upper Paintbrush Canyon

Paintbrush Canyon

Just to the west of Leigh Lake, and accessible from the String Lake Trailhead, sits Paintbrush Canyon. Fifteen thousand years ago Paintbrush Canyon held one of the glaciers that created Leigh Lake. The trail crosses a bridge where String Lake meets Leigh Lake and contours up and around through conifers into Paintbrush Canyon. The only big canyon oriented more to the north and south, it offers a slightly different exposure to weather, the sun, and summer sunsets. The trail climbs moderately uphill all the way, with lots of viewpoints and some nice established camp sites. Panoramic views of Leigh and Jackson lakes spread out below. The trail climbs more steeply as it goes, winding up through stands of Subalpine Fir, boulder fields, and scree. Eventually it reaches Holly Lake in a wide cirque below Mt. Woodring. Holly Lake is surrounded by alpine wildflowers, big boulders, and fantastic scenery. From Holly Lake, the trail climbs up and over Paintbrush Divide to Lake Solitude and down Cascade Canyon.

Canyons without Well-Maintained Trails

Some canyons in the Tetons are not a part of the park's marked and maintained trail system, and the National Park Service recommends only experienced hikers and climbers visit them. However, they offer views into the mountain range and have geologic highlights that can be observed from vantage points in the valley below.

Avalanche Canyon

Avalanche Canyon from Taggart Lake

Mountain climbers use Avalanche Canyon primarily for access to routes on several adjacent peaks, and few hikers go there. From the valley it offers outstanding views deep into the mountain range, both from turnouts along the park highways and from the trails near Taggart and Bradley Lakes. Avalanche Canyon creates some moody, visual effects on the Teton landscape as afternoon storms linger within its walls and dark thunderstorms and low rain clouds pass through the canyon. Storms highlight some of the nearby peaks and obscure others, giving a dramatic perspective to the mountains. When the weather passes and the late afternoon sun reappears, it may send brilliant shafts of light directly down Avalanche Canyon. Shoshoko Falls, high up in the canyon, can be seen from Taggart Lake, as well as a large limestone formation walling off the head of the canyon.

Glacier Gulch

Glacier Gulch separates the Grand Teton from Mount Owen, just to the north. The Teton Glacier sits high in the canyon, and in the early 1920s there were regular visits to the glacier by horseback parties. The trail was not among those developed and maintained when the park was established. A roadside viewpoint named "Teton Glacier Turnout" on the road to Jenny Lake, and another called "Glacier View Turnout" on highway 89/191 on the east side of the valley offer spectacular views into Glacier Gulch. Hiking up to Amphitheater and Surprise lakes and looking over the edge to the north gives you an intimate view of Glacier Gulch.

Teton Glacier and Glacier Gulch (left)

Hanging Canyon

Hanging Canyon

The high, shallow canyon rising from the west shore of Jenny Lake, to the right of Cascade Canyon, and leading up into the peaks is Hanging Canyon. Symmetry Spire is on its left side and Mount St. John is on the right. This is an extremely rugged little canyon and has no regular trail, but it is an important piece of the landscape as seen from the lakeshore trails around Jenny and String Lakes.

Leigh Canyon

Leigh Canyon

Due west of Leigh Lake lies Leigh Canyon, and together with Paintbrush Canyon, held the glaciers that carved Leigh Lake. Leigh Canyon divides Mount Moran to the north from Mount Woodring to the south. It offers great views into the mountains from the east shore of Leigh Lake or from one of the campsites at the west end of the lake.

Moran Canyon

Moran Canyon from across Jackson Lake

Mount Moran dominates the Teton skyline from Leigh Lake all the way to the north end of Jackson Lake. Sitting on the north side of Mt. Moran to accent the massive peak is Moran Canyon. Great views of the canyon exist from across Jackson Lake at Signal Mountain, from Hermitage Point, or from Colter Bay. Moran Canyon never fails to add dramatic atmosphere to the Tetons with storms, rays of sunshine, or a clear view to the western sky at sundown.

View of Moran Canyon from Signal Mountain (right)

Lakes of the Valley

The glaciers that shaped this park many thousands of years ago left a string of beautiful lakes along the base of the Teton Range. Most were made by large glaciers that pushed out of the mountain canyons and left deep depressions that were further dammed by moraines. Other lakes formed in basins scooped out by massive glaciers that moved through the valley. Like the peaks and canyons of the mountains, the lakes of Grand Teton are easily accessible and are a natural part of the landscape.

Phelps Lake

This beautiful lake, named for trapper and hunter George Phelps, hides behind one of the highest and most obvious moraines in the park. Located at the mouth of Death Canyon, Phelps Lake makes a perfect place to appreciate the sheer beauty of a glacier-carved land.

You access Phelps Lake from the Death Canyon Trailhead. Just under a mile of fairly easy hiking brings you to the Phelps Lake Overlook, with panoramic views of the lake and Death Canyon. Another mile down a steep, switchback trail gets you to the lake level where there's a small campground. The trail continues on to Death Canyon and Open Canyon.

The lake provides excellent fishing for trout from the shore, and the rugged east side usually proves productive. There's also fishing access near the inlet, where Death Creek enters. Swimmers describe the lake as "exhilarating"—clear and cold. The lake turns shallow and sandy at the inlet end. An established lakeshore campground, with permits available by reservation, sits in the forest at the north end.

Moose inhabit the thickets and forest at the canyon end of the lake, and mule deer can be seen early and late anywhere around the lake. Birds are plentiful in the vegetation along the shores and near the trail from the overlook. Death Canyon and the Phelps Lake area always seem to have a few black bears.

At the far end of the lake lies the historic J-Y Ranch, one of the first dude ranches in the valley, built in 1908. It attracted wealthy eastern clients, including such notable dudes as author Owen Wister and his family, until the Rockefeller's Snake River Land Company bought the ranch in 1932. The J-Y's dude ranch era ended, but the property remained with the Rockefeller family, and they used it as a summer retreat for many years. In the early 2000s the family donated it to Grand Teton National Park.

Phelps Lake (left)

Taggart Lake

Always a popular destination, Taggart Lake waits not far from the trailhead and offers great views of the high peaks and up into Avalanche Canyon. It was named for geologist W. Rush Taggart of the 1872 Hayden Expedition. The Taggart Lake Trailhead accesses it, about 1.5 miles one way, and it climbs over a moraine formed by the glacier that shaped Avalanche Canyon. The moraine was burned clear by forest fires in 1985, and lush new growth now covers it.

Fishing for trout from shore attracts anglers all year, especially early in the summer. Swimming is permitted, but the cold water and the rocky shore discourage most hikers from trying. With the beautiful view across the lake to the mountains changing by the hour, this is a good area for photography and painting.

Moose inhabit the moraine year-round. Mule deer are often seen along the creek just off the trail, early and late in the day. Many species of birds inhabit the burn area and Lodgepole Pine forest near the lake.

Taggart Lake makes a good hike for children, with an easy loop back on a different trail, and Bradley Lake is close by for a slightly longer hike.

Bradley Lake

Bradley Lake

The second in a pair of lakes, Bradley Lake is a bit smaller and more enclosed by trees than Taggart. Named for Hayden's chief geologist, Frank Bradley, it's just up the trail a mile from Taggart. It lies at the base of Garnet Canyon, surrounded by the moraine. At its east end a marshy area with ponds formed where the outlet flows. Moose can usually be found nearby.

The Taggart Lake Trailhead provides access, or you can hike in on the trail into Garnet Canyon from Lupine Meadows Trailhead. Even though it's so close to Taggart Lake and Garnet Canyon, few people go there.

Unlike members of most government survey expeditions of the 1800s, the geologists of the Hayden Expedition didn't tend to name things after themselves. These two lakes were an exception, with Frank Bradley and his assistant, William Taggart, each receiving the honor of a small lake bearing their name. Interestingly, today the trail to these two lakes is a popular hike for teaching basic geology of the Teton landscape.

The Grand Teton reflected in Taggart Lake (right)

String Lake

String Lake

This clear, shallow lake looks more like a wide channel between Leigh Lake and Jenny Lake. It sits right against the steep lower slopes of Mount St. John and Rockchuck Peak. Periodic avalanches have kept the slopes clear of trees.

String Lake made a name early on as the place to swim in Grand Teton National Park. Beginning in the early 1900s, guests at historic dude ranches and early homesteaders all enjoyed the water of String Lake. Its shallow, clear water is relatively warm, and the sandy bottom makes it especially inviting. The improved picnic area provides enough space for groups and is a favorite locals' spot. Canoeists and kayakers launch their boats here on the way to Leigh Lake.

Waterfowl like the shallow water and protective vegetation at the south end, near the footbridge to the Jenny Lake Loop Trail. Dippers and Harlequin Ducks are two interesting species seen here. Sandhill Cranes nest in the marsh across the lake, opposite the trail to Leigh Lake. Moose are commonly seen on the far shore, and deer and black bears feed on the steep slopes.

Leigh Lake

Leigh Lake

One of the prettiest lakes in the park, Leigh Lake has a sandy eastern shore and postcard views across to Mount Moran and into Leigh and Paintbrush Canyons. Melting glacier ice helps color the water. Leigh Lake reaches about 250 feet in depth.

Leigh Lake can be reached from the Leigh Lake Trailhead at the String Lake parking area, an easy and scenic one-mile walk. It's another mile to the middle of the east shoreline for the best views. You can also paddle a canoe a mile up to the end of String Lake for a short portage across land to Leigh Lake.

Leigh Lake offers just about everything in the way of recreation: camping among the pine trees on the lakeshore, canoeing across the lake, trout fishing, and swimming in the shallow east side. Five campsites are designed for canoe access, with three on the scenic east shoreline. The three eastern sites

Bearpaw Lake

are close to the trail and will have hikers passing by during the day.

Moose, deer, and an occasional black bear will be seen on the shores of the lake. Loons, ducks, and geese visit the lake. There are Gray Jays, kinglets, and other small birds along the shoreline trail.

Leigh Lake was originally one of the prime destinations in the park. The first superintendent built a road to the south end of the lake before the idea was abandoned and the land reclaimed. Traces of the road can still be seen between Leigh Lake and String Lake.

Bearpaw Lake and Trapper Lake

This pair of small lakes lies hidden in the trees just past Leigh Lake. They offer solitude, fishing, and a chance to escape the crowds without going too far into the backcountry. The Leigh Lake Trailhead provides access at the String Lake parking area. These lakes offer camping and fishing and are sometimes available for overnight when the popular Leigh Lake campsites are all reserved.

Mount Moran reflected in String Lake (overleaf)

Jackson Lake

By far the largest body of water in the park, Jackson Lake was scraped out by massive glaciers from the north about 15,000 years ago. The original basin was about 800 feet deep. Glacial sediment gradually filled in the basin to make the present lake bottom at 400 feet. The west shore hugs the steep base of the Tetons, and the east shore is characterized by tree-covered moraines, bays, and islands. Jackson Lake can be extremely picturesque, with several key spots for viewing it: the summit of Signal Mountain, Colter Bay, and a series of turnouts along the road toward Yellowstone Park.

Jackson Lake is accessible by car at numerous points. Marinas at Signal Mountain, Leeks Lodge, and Colter Bay provide access for boats, and rent canoes and small motorboats. Small boats can be launched at Spalding Bay and at various sites along the north end of the lake during higher water. Hiking trails from Jackson Lake Lodge and Colter Bay explore the interesting topography along the eastern shore.

Engineers built a dam at the outlet of Jackson Lake in 1910 and 1911 to store irrigation water for Idaho farmers downstream. This dam raised the water level 39 feet, enlarging the lake by one-third and flooding the surrounding forests. (One of the great achievements of the Civilian Conser-

Looking south from the north end of Jackson Lake

vation Corps in the 1930s was cutting up and removing all the trees killed by flooding.) Now, as the water is released to Idaho and lake levels drop during summer months, the water gets warmer and the lake becomes even more popular.

Jackson Lake evolved as the center of summer water recreation in the park, with great boating, swimming, water-skiing, fishing, camping, and sightseeing. Although boating remains the prime sport, and most camping and fishing spots are best reached over water, many options exist for the non-boater. Fishing is excellent—in fact, a record 50-pound lake trout was caught from shore—and campsites are available along the eastern shore.

Just about every species of park wildlife inhabits the area around Jackson Lake. The shallow north end of the lake provides a haven for waterfowl, and its willow flats and marshes are home to moose. Elk and deer are common in the hills above the lake all along the east side. Moose are almost a certainty in the willow flats, ponds, and meadows that surround Jackson Lake Lodge. Black bears are often seen between the Jackson Lake Dam and Signal Mountain. Eagles and Ospreys inhabit the area near the dam and are seen often in most of the bays.

Emma Matilda Lake

Emma Matilda Lake and Two Ocean Lake

These two lakes sit almost side by side just east of Jackson Lake, in basins scraped out by earlier glacier activity than the ice that made the park's other lakes. Although farther from the mountains and off the main path, these two lakes offer an ideal place to get away for a day.

Emma Matilda was the name of the wife of William Owen, the man credited with the first successful climb of the Grand Teton. Two Ocean Lake is probably named for nearby Two Ocean Plateau, which sits on the Continental Divide and whose streams eventually drain into both oceans.

Access is via the gravel Pacific Creek Road that follows that creek from the highway near Moran Junction. A few miles up the road you turn north (left) on the side road marked Two Ocean Lake. The trail loops around Two Ocean Lake and hops over the moraine to skirt Emma Matilda on the way to Jackson Lake Lodge. Both lakes can be reached on foot from Jackson Lake Lodge or from the Grand View Point Trailhead.

Both lakes offer good fishing, and Two Ocean Lake can be fished from a canoe. There are moose, deer, elk, and both grizzly and black bears inhabiting the area. Both lakes are ideal places for bird-watching.

View from Emma Matilda Lake trail (left)

Amphitheater Lake

Lakes of the Mountains

Although many little lakes dot the high country in the Tetons, only a few are accessible by maintained trails. Because of the very fragile nature of alpine lakes and their surrounding vegetation, park managers discourage visiting the more remote lakes except by experienced backcountry hikers with an understanding of alpine ecology.

The following lakes, however, can be reached by park trails and offer a comprehensive array of alpine lake features.

Surprise Lake and Amphitheater Lake

Surprise Lake

The rounded, steep ridge that seems to lead straight up from the valley floor to the Grand Teton doesn't actually reach the summit. It gets cut off by a sheer drop three-fourths of the way up, to form Disappointment Peak. But just at timberline, where the trees give way to rock, two small lakes, Surprise Lake and Amphitheater Lake, sit in cirques carved out by glaciers.

From Lupine Meadows, take the trail toward Garnet Canyon. This trail forks off to the lakes, and you follow the signs to the right. It's 4.5 miles and all uphill, 3,000 feet. These lakes are popular, but not all who start out on the trail get there.

These lakes provide fantastic views. The trail leading up to the lakes has switchbacks all the way, offering a variety of views out over the valley. Picturesque settings, with wind-shaped trees, snow and ice, wildflowers, and the peaks above make this destination unforgettable.

Lake Solitude

Lake Solitude and the Grand Teton

The largest lake accessible by trail is Lake Solitude. Its classic view of the backs of the Grand Teton, Mount Owen, and Teewinot Mountain makes it a popular destination. Solitude sits behind a glacial moraine in a large cirque at the head of Cascade Canyon. Cascade Creek originates here. Trees are sparse at this elevation, over 9,000 feet, but alpine wildflowers are abundant.

The Cascade Canyon Trail follows the scenic canyon to Lake Solitude, nine miles from Jenny Lake parking area and seven from the West Shore Boat Dock. Although Cascade Canyon has a gentle grade, the trail gets steeper close to the lake.

The views, especially for artists or photographers, are tremendous. Camping by permit exists along the trail just below the lake's moraine and provides a chance to watch sunrise or sunset at the lake. Camping here is also a means of experiencing, after day-hikers have gone, the feeling that gave the lake its name.

Marion Lake

Holly Lake

This classic little cirque lake in Paintbrush Canyon makes a perfect destination for a more strenuous picnic hike. The trail climbs steadily uphill but offers numerous places to rest and take in the view. A little over six miles from the Leigh Lake Trailhead, Holly Lake makes a fairly difficult destination because of steady elevation gain. Paintbrush Canyon is less visited than Cascade Canyon, and it's easier to get away from everyone. The increasingly steeper trail as you near the lake turns some visitors back, so that the lake itself is often deserted. If you make it, you'll find beautiful mountain views, alpine trees, and abundant wildflowers.

Marion Lake, Basin Lakes, and Sunset Lake

For the hiker wanting to experience some of the tiny lakes set in the alpine tundra, these lakes are accessible by the Teton Crest Trail. The lakes are less dramatic, but they sit in some of the greatest wild scenery in the park.

Holly Lake (left)   *High in the Teton backcountry (overleaf)*

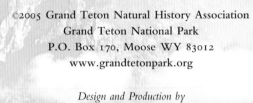

©2005 Grand Teton Natural History Association
Grand Teton National Park
P.O. Box 170, Moose WY 83012
www.grandtetonpark.org

Design and Production by
Jeff Pollard Design & Associates

Maps by
Mike Reagan

Project Coordinated by
Jan Lynch, Executive Director,
Grand Teton Natural History Association

Printed by
Paragon Press

ISBN 0-931895-60-X